J
BIO
SHEERAN

Orr, Tamra

Ed Sheeran

A BEACON ✦ BIOGRAPHY

ED
SHEERAN

Tamra Orr

PURPLE TOAD
PUBLISHING

PURPLE TOAD
PUBLISHING

Printing   1   2   3   4   5   6   7   8   9

A Beacon Biography

Angelina Jolie
Big Time Rush
Carly Rae Jepsen
Drake
Ed Sheeran
Harry Styles of One Direction
Jennifer Lawrence
Kevin Durant
Lorde
Malala
Markus "Notch" Persson, Creator of Minecraft
Mo'ne Davis
Muhammad Ali
Neil deGrasse Tyson
Peyton Manning
Robert Griffin III (RG3)

Publisher's Cataloging-in-Publication Data
Orr, Tamra.
   Ed Sheeran / written by Tamra Orr.
     p. cm.
            Includes bibliographic references and index.
            ISBN 9781624692505
1. Sheeran, Ed, 1991—Juvenile literature. 2. Singers—England—Biography—Juvenile literature. I. Series: Beacon Biographies Collection Two.
  ML3930.S484 2016
  782.42164092

                                                    Library of Congress Control Number: 2015941816

eBook ISBN: 9781624692512

ABOUT THE AUTHOR: Tamra Orr is a full-time author living in the Pacific Northwest. She has written more than 400 educational books for readers of all ages. She is a graduate of Ball State University and commonly gives presentations to schools and conferences. Since she is the mother of four, she has done her best to keep up with all current music groups. Unlike some of the groups she has encountered, listening to and learning about Ed Sheeran has been a pleasure. She likes his smile almost as much as she likes his music.

PUBLISHER'S NOTE: The data in this book has been researched in depth, and to the best of our knowledge is factual. Although every measure is taken to give an accurate account, Purple Toad Publishing makes no warranty of the accuracy of the information and is not liable for damages caused by inaccuracies. This story has not been authorized or endorsed by Ed Sheeran.

CONTENTS

Chapter 1

Alone in London

From an early age, Sheeran knew exactly what he wanted to do with his life—make music. Now, how to get started?

It seemed like a great plan at the time. Ed Sheeran loved writing and playing music. He knew it. His family and friends knew it. Now he wanted more of the world to know it also. He packed his backpack, grabbed his guitar, and prepared to head out the door to London.

When Sheeran decided it was time to leave home, his father was one of his biggest supporters. "My dad said, 'If you really want to do it, don't have a fallback plan. Because you eventually will do it if there's no other option,'" Sheeran recalled in an interview with *FT Magazine*. "But mum wasn't too keen on the idea."[1]

When Sheeran got to London, he enrolled in a course called Access to Music. This gave him enough grant money to pay his rent—but only for a while. When the money ran out, so did having a place to stay. Suddenly, Sheeran found himself on the street. His plan to become a famous musician was a bit harder when he was not sure where he would find a meal or a place to sleep each night.

In Sheeran's book, *Ed Sheeran: A Visual Journey* (2014), he writes about those lonely days in London. He told *The Daily Mail*, "I didn't have anywhere to live for much of 2008 and the

Sleeping on the train wasn't the most comfortable way to do it, but it got Sheeran through some of the toughest times in London.

whole of 2009 and 2010, but somehow I made it work. I knew where I could get a bed at a certain time of night and I knew who I could call at any time to get a floor to sleep on."[2]

"I wasn't really homeless," he continued. "Not proper cardboard box stuff. But yeah, I would gig at night and if I didn't have a sofa to crash on, I'd sleep on the Circle Line [train] all day. Then I'd gig the following night and do it all again."[3] He would get on the subway train at 5 a.m. and sleep on it until noon, and then head out to do another performance, day after day.

In an interview with *The Guardian*, Sheeran admitted those days were rough at times. "I mean, at the end of the day, I was enjoying doing it," he said. "I would have done it whether it worked out or didn't. But there were definitely moments that weren't great."[4] He told reporter Elizabeth Day that it was extremely tiring to have to sell enough CDs out of his backpack to buy train tickets and food for the night.

Not Giving Up

One thing that Sheeran was, however, was determined. He was not going to go back home, but decided he would play at every possible gig he could. He told a reporter from MTV, "There were moments I wanted to give up. The nights that you don't have a couch to sleep on, or you don't have money in your pocket, or food in your stomach or a charged phone. Those become the nights where you reassess your situation."[5]

Sheeran would sometimes nap in a heated arch just outside London's famous Buckingham Palace. In 2012, he walked right back through that same arch to play at the sold-out Queen's Diamond Jubilee Concert. There he performed the song he wrote, "Homeless," inspired by his nights sleeping outside the palace. After the concert, Sheeran shook hands with Queen Elizabeth—an event he most likely could not have imagined when he had been sleeping outside the palace years earlier. What a difference a couple of years can make!

Even the Queen came out to see Sheeran play!

Sheeran battled a number of problems as a little boy, but each one only made him stronger.

The Rap Solution

When Edward Christopher Sheeran picked up his first guitar, it was clear that he had found his purpose in life—even if he was only a kid. He had been singing in the church choir for years, so he knew he liked music. But a guitar gave him the chance to *make* music. "I first picked up a guitar when I was 10 or 11," he told *Independent* reporter Andy Welch. "I picked up a few chords and quite quickly started writing my own songs using other people's chord structures," he explained. "By the time I was 14 or so, I thought music was something I'd like to do, and then by 16, I started to think it was something I could do."[1]

A Weird Child

Sheeran was born on February 17, 1991 in Halifax, England. He describes himself as an odd kid. "I was a very, very weird child," he admits.[2] He wore big, thick blue glasses. He had a large, dark birthmark on his face. He was missing an eardrum in one of his ears. To top it all off, he had developed a stutter. "The thing I found most difficult was knowing what to say but not really [being] able to express it the right way," he said in a 2015 speech to the American Institute for Stuttering. "Stuttering is not a thing you have to be worried about at all," he told the crowd. "Even if you have quirks and weirdness, you shouldn't be worried about that."[3]

In an interview with *The Hollywood Reporter* after the benefit, Sheeran added, "Having things that make you different help you become an interesting person. Most of the people I knew that were normal in school are all pretty dull right now. . . . Most of the people that are successful started life off as a weird kid with no friends."[4]

Family Rules

Sheeran's mother, Imogen, is a jewelry designer, and his father, John, is an art curator. His older brother, Matt, is a composer. He writes the soundtracks for many wildlife documentaries. The two brothers have tried writing music together, but their different styles do not mesh well. In an interview with *FT Magazine*, Sheeran stated, "[Matt] does a completely different thing. It's a clash of minds. Matt's more classically trained."[5]

Ed with mother, Imogen

The entire family loves music. The parents were less fond of electronics, however. They strictly limited the amount of television the Sheeran kids were allowed to watch. In fact, according to Ed in a *Daily Mail* interview, "for years we didn't have a TV in the house."[6] Game systems were not allowed in the house, either. Sheeran admits, "I still don't know what to do with an Xbox. On our tour bus, everyone's playing . . . and I kind of wish I could play it, but I have no clue what to do."[7]

When Sheeran's father realized his son was struggling with his stutter, he bought the nine-year-old something unusual to help: *The Marshall Mathers LP* by Eminem. Sheeran memorized the entire rap album. "I learned every word of it," he told *The Hollywood Reporter,* "back to front, by the time I was ten.

John Sheeran with son Ed

He [Eminem] raps very fast and melodically and percussively, and it helped me get rid of the stutter."[8]

Sheeran's experience with stuttering affected him in many ways. He offers advice for young people who struggle to clearly express themselves: "Just be yourself, because there's no one in the world that can be a better you than you," he says. "Embrace your quirks. Being weird is a wonderful thing. . . .Embrace your weirdness."[9]

Sheeran also struggled at Thomas Mills High School in Framlingham, Suffolk. If he could not immediately see the purpose of what he was learning, he lost interest in studying it. In an interview with *The Telegraph,* Sheeran described the conflict: "My dad always used to [punish] me for not working hard. And it wasn't that—it's just that I didn't see any point in working hard for those particular things. As soon as I found music, that's what I worked hard at. . . .There were just certain things that seemed pointless. So I never really applied myself."[10]

Although the stage seems very empty when Sheeran performs, his fans know he can fill it up with his unique and exciting music.

Chapter

3

From the U.K. to the U.S.

Before Sheeran packed his bags for London, he was writing songs. His first extended-play album (EP) was *The Orange Room*. It was released in May 2005 when he only 14 years old. It featured five songs. After Sheeran got to the city, he focused on one thing: performing as many times and places as possible. "I played 312 shows in 2009," he said in an interview with *The Independent*. "Sometimes to no one, or five people, often to more."[1]

Sheeran followed this EP with 2006's *Ed Sheeran*, 2007's *Want Some?* and 2009's *You Need Me, I Don't Need You*. Each of these EPs was released independently. Sheeran did not have an agent. No record label had hired him yet. He sold his music through performing on the streets and in pubs, bars, cafés, and nightclubs.

His first big year was 2010. Early in the year, he released a video for "You Need Me, I Don't Need You" online. Rapper Example happened to see it and was impressed. He asked Sheeran to go on tour with him as his opening performer at concerts. The young musician agreed. At the same time, he

Sheeran was inspired by his time working at the homeless shelter and the people he met there.

released another independent EP called *Loose Change.* It included a hit single called "The A Team." This song was inspired by a personal experience Sheeran had while working at a homeless shelter. "I have a friend who works at a homeless shelter every Christmas," he explained in an interview with *The Independent.* "He asked me to go along one year and play some songs for the people there." While he was there, Sheeran met a young woman named Angel. Her story deeply saddened him. "I learned a lot about Angel, the unfortunate ways she earned her money on the street, and the things she did with it when she had it—it was a very bleak story. I spent some time with her playing her favorite songs, and then wrote 'The A Team' for her."[2] The record sold hundreds of thousands of copies over the year.

In April 2010, Sheeran made a huge decision. He decided to go to the United States. In Los Angeles, just as he had in London, he began playing as many gigs as he could. Within a few months, his career was taking off so fast it shocked even him. First actor, rapper, and producer Jamie Foxx heard his music and got in touch. He invited Sheeran to appear on his radio show. He also offered his personal recording studio for Sheeran's use. "I got on with him really well and hung out for a bit. He's just a really, really nice dude," Sheeran told a BBC reporter.[3]

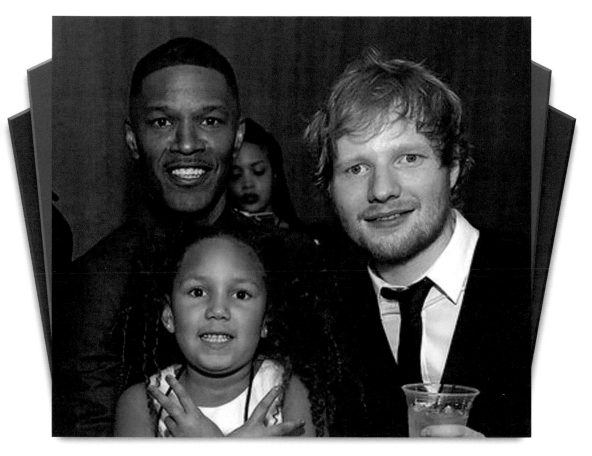

Sheeran became a close friend to Jamie Foxx, and spent time with him and his daughter Annalise.

Sheeran's music was on YouTube, and he released two more independent EPs, *Ed Sheeran: Live at the Bedford* and *Songs I Wrote with Amy.* It was his next EP, however, that made all the difference.

In the Mainstream

In 2011, Sheeran released yet another independent EP. This one was called *No. 5 Collaborations Project.* It featured a number of guest artists and soon reached number 2 on the iTunes chart. It sold thousands of copies in the first week. By the end of April, Sheeran had what so many musicians dreamed of—a contract with Atlantic Records.

The redhead found so much success in the U.S. that even he was startled.

Sheeran and Swift are good friends only, as Ed described the two as "cast members of 'The Hobbit.' She's like, in the elven kingdom," Sheeran said. "She's hanging out with Galadriel and stuff, and I've got hairy feet."[4]

His first full album, +, (referred to as *Plus*) was released and was a huge hit. One million copies were sold in the United Kingdom (U.K.). As his songs were played on the radio, Sheeran was also writing songs for other artists to perform, including the group One Direction and for singer Taylor Swift. He and Swift became close friends, and he helped her write several songs that were released on her 2012 album, *Red.* The video for one of them, their duet "Everything Has Changed," was released on June 6, 2013. Two years later, the video was still a big hit, with more than 138 million views on YouTube.

From this point on, Sheeran's career as a musician has shot straight up like a rocket. It is a flight that, so far, has shown no signs of slowing down.

Sheeran's image on stage is incredibly simple, from his clothing to his guitar. It allows his music to shine.

Astounding Success

Watching Ed Sheeran's rise from a kid playing on the corner in London to a superstar performing in some of the world's largest venues is nothing short of astounding. His climb to fame has been one of the fastest in music history. Even though some critics have penned some rough reviews of his songs, his fan base has continued to grow and grow—and that is what it is all about for Sheeran.

"Everything I do is for my fans," he admitted in an interview with *The Independent*. "I don't make music for the critics. They didn't spend a tenner [money] on my album, they haven't come to my shows for the past few years. A lot of those guys probably listened to my album once or twice and that was that. . . . Well, I don't care what they think," he adds. "If a fan came up and said they didn't like what I'd done, then it would hit me and I'd take it in and think about it. Obviously not everyone is going to like what I do, but things seem to be going pretty well so far."[1]

"Pretty well" is an understatement.

In 2012, he won the Best British Solo Male artist award, as well as the British Breakthrough Act of the Year. In addition, his song "The A Team" won the Ivor Novello Music Award for Best Song

Sheeran says Paul McCartney and The Beatles are some of his influences.

Musically and Lyrically. This songwriting award is held in high respect in the music world. "This award is run by songwriters, voted on by songwriters—like Paul McCartney would be on the panel," Sheeran explained to *Entertainment Weekly.*[2] The song was also nominated for Best Song of the Year in the 2013 Grammy Awards.

Sheeran went on tour with the pop hit group Snow Patrol. He also went on Taylor Swift's The Red Tour in 2013. His songs began appearing in hit television shows such as *The Vampire Diaries* and *Cougar Town.* Along with appearing in front of Queen Elizabeth, Sheeran also appeared in the closing ceremony for the 2012 Summer Olympics, singing Pink Floyd's "Wish You Were Here." In addition, his song "I See Fire" was played during the ending credits and in the soundtrack of the blockbuster movie *The Hobbit: The Desolation of Smaug.*

The Next Album

In June 2014, Sheeran released his next album, *X*, or *Multiply.* According to Sheeran in an interview with *Entertainment Weekly,* "*Multiply* was called *Multiply* because it made everything that was on *Plus* bigger, from the venues to the songs to the radio plays to the sales."[3] This album included the hit single "Thinking Out Loud." In the official music video, a thinner Ed Sheeran appears as a dance partner in the middle of a ballroom. He shares the dance floor with Brittany Cherry, a finalist from the television show *So You Think You Can Dance* and a cast member on *Dancing with the Stars.* In the first

The image of a well-dressed, romantic, and dancing Sheeran grabbed the attention of millions of fans online.

24 hours it was posted online, the video had been viewed almost three million times. The song also set a chart record in the U.K.: it was the first single to spend a full year in the U.K.'s Top 40. *Multiply* spent a full year in the U.K.'s Top Ten Albums.[4] It was also a huge hit in the United States, peaking at number 2 on the Billboard 100.

Preparing for the dancing part of the video took a lot of work. "If you put your mind to anything, you can do it," Sheeran said to *EW* reporter James Hibberd. "So I had three weeks and two very, very capable dancers and teachers on tour with me, and we just practiced five hours a day."[5]

A number of the songs Sheeran has written over the years have been about the musician's personal experiences or acquaintances. The songs help him work through his feelings and reactions. In an interview with *The Independent*, Sheeran said, "For me, though, writing personal songs is like therapy, just to get it all out. That's my justification for writing it, and my justification on releasing it is that there might be someone out there who feels the same way."[6]

Sheeran's fan base has multiplied to fill entire stadiums.

Playing It Forward

By the time Sheeran was 24 years old, he had already earned a very long list of awards. The list of nominations was even longer. While Sheeran has enjoyed the money he earns, he has not gone wild over it. When one of his first songs reached number one, he celebrated by buying himself a LEGO® Star Wars™ Millennium Falcon toy. "I'm not very materialistic," he says, "but I enjoyed making that."[1]

In July 2015, Ed Sheeran sold out three nights in a row at Wembley Stadium, a soccer stadium in London that holds 93,000 people. He was the first performer to entertain that many people in that location—as a solo act. No band. No other singers. No dancers. Just Sheeran on the stage. Of course, he had quite a few exciting opening acts lined up to entertain the crowd, including OneRepublic, rapper Example, and Northern Irishman Foy Vance. "I actually sorted the support acts before I'd even put [the tickets] on sale," he told *Gigwise*. "I've got three acts every day, and they're all multiplatinum. . . . They're all great, they're all really, really good"[2]

He had a huge surprise in store as well: Joining him onstage for "Don't Go Breaking My Heart" was none other than Sir Elton

Elton John joined Sheeran on stage at Wembley Stadium to play piano. Together they sang an Elton John hit—and then one of Sheeran's.

John. When critics came to review the concert, many thought Sheeran was the most foolish—however brave—performer they had ever seen. Standing up in front of almost one hundred thousand people armed with nothing more than a guitar and a microphone seemed like a recipe for disaster. Instead it was a charming success. The audience was thrilled—and the stadium was full every night.

In spring 2015, he announced that he was launching his own record label. In honor of his bright red curly hair, he named it Gingerbread. He wants to use the label to help other new and unknown artists get the incredible chances to succeed that he did. The first artist he signed is Jamie Lawson, from Plymouth, U.K. "There are people on that scene who make me look terrible by just being so good," he told *Gigwise*. "They haven't got the right platform. I have a tour and Twitter, so I can put them in front of my fans instantly," he continued. "I can sit down with heads of radio stations and ask whether they'll play it on the radio. I'm in a really fortunate position to be able to break acts."[3]

Sharing the Success

Another trait Sheeran is known for is his kindness. Over the years, he has accepted a marriage proposal from a fan with terminal cancer, serenaded a seriously ill fan over the phone, and donated all of his stage and photo-shoot clothes to local thrift stores. He has allowed fans at his concerts to come up on stage and propose to their partners. He has surprised big fans by showing up without warning to perform a song.

In 2014, Sheeran wrote a book about his life to date. Called *Ed Sheeran: A Visual Journey*, it was illustrated by one of his childhood friends, Phillip Butah. It has over 100 photographs and illustrations in it.

What advice does Sheeran have for young people who want to follow in his musical footsteps? He told *Interview* magazine, "I would say, you can never do enough gigs and you can never do enough songs. Make sure that every opportunity you can, play a show and every opportunity you can, write a song. The more you write tunes, the better they will become. The more you do gigs, the better you will become. . . . Keep your fingers crossed, start from the bottom and work your way up."[4]

If anyone knows how to get better, Sheeran does. He keeps doing it every day.

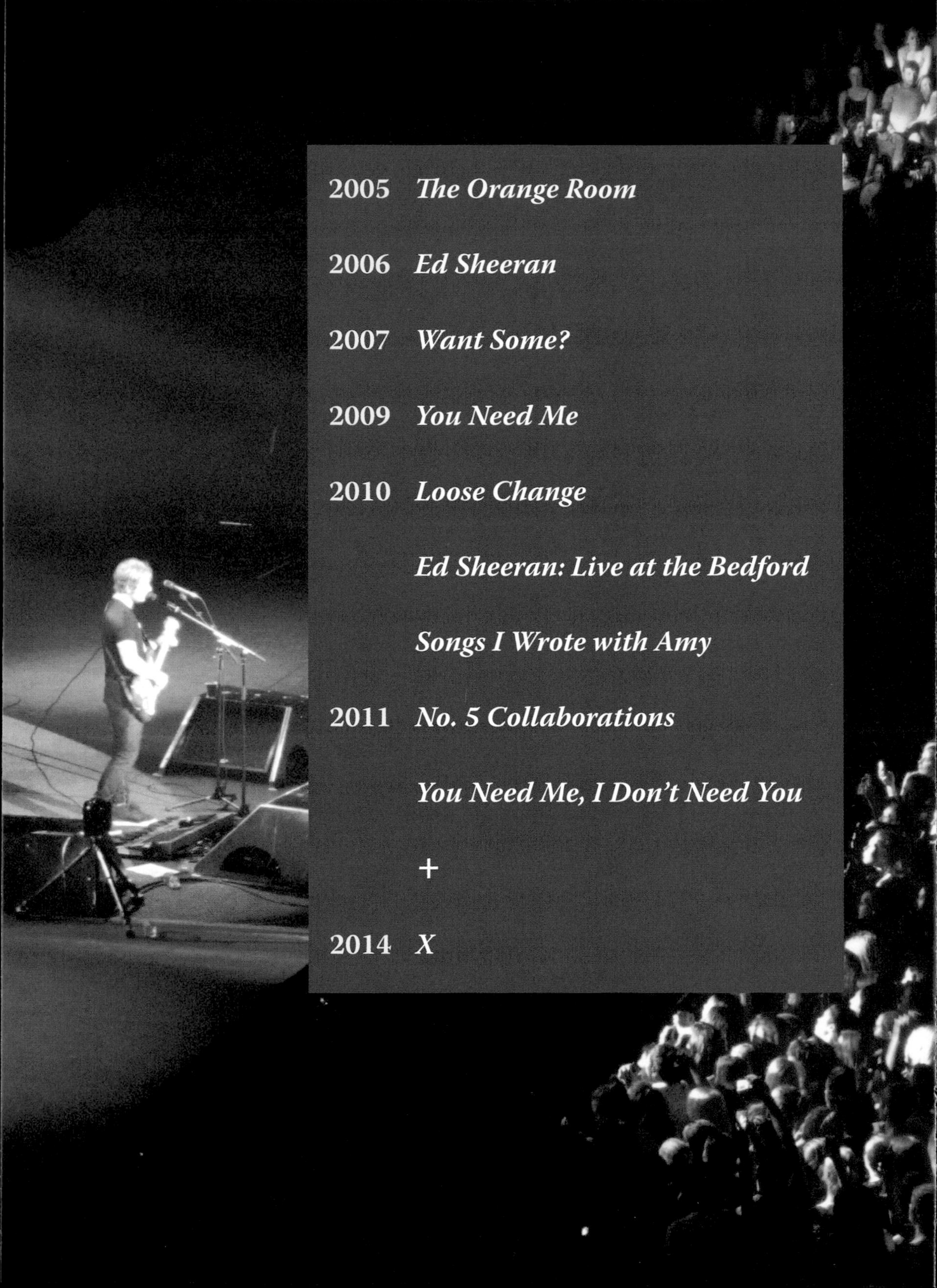

2005   *The Orange Room*

2006   *Ed Sheeran*

2007   *Want Some?*

2009   *You Need Me*

2010   *Loose Change*

        Ed Sheeran: Live at the Bedford

        Songs I Wrote with Amy

2011   *No. 5 Collaborations*

        You Need Me, I Don't Need You

        +

2014   *X*

1991 Edward Christopher Sheeran is born on February 17 in Halifax, England.

2000 His parents buy him *The Marshall Mathers LP* by Eminem to help him overcome his stutter.

2005 He releases his first EP, *The Orange Room*.

2010 He releases a video online, which catches the attention of rapper Example. His single "The A Team" is released, spotlighting homeless youth. He goes to Los Angeles.

2011 *No. 5 Collaborations Project* reaches No. 2 on the iTunes chart. Atlantic Records signs Sheeran to a contract. He writes songs with Taylor Swift for her album *Red*.

2012 He receives Best British Solo Male Artist Award and the British Breakthrough Act of the Year. "The A Team" wins the Ivor Novello Music Award for Best Song Musically and Lyrically.

2013 Sheeran tours with Snow Patrol and with Taylor Swift on her Red Tour. Swift and Sheeran's "Everything Has Changed" video is released. Sheeran's songs receive play on TV series.

2014 *X (Multiply)* is released. It includes the hit single "Thinking Out Loud." The illustrated autobiography *Ed Sheeran: A Visual Journey* is published.

2015 In May, Sheeran announces the launch of his record label, Gingerbread. In July, he performs in three sold-out shows in London's Wembley Stadium. He releases his single "Growing Up (Sloan's Song)"—and it's free. It is a collaboration with Macklemore & Lewis

Chapter 1. Alone in London

1. Craig McLean, "The Business of Being Ed Sheeran," *FT Magazine*, December 19, 2014. http://www.ft.com/intl/cms/s/2/0b124842-856a-11e4-ab4e-00144feabdc0.html

2. Chris Hastings, "Popstar Ed Sheeran Reveals: I Slept Outside Buckingham Palace and Was Homeless for Two Years," *The Daily Mail*, October 11, 2014. http://www.dailymail.co.uk/tvshowbiz/article-2789411/popstar-ed-sheeran-reveals-slept-outside-buckingham-palace-homeless-two-years.html

3. Ibid.

4. Elizabeth Day, "Ed Sheeran: 'I Got Quite a Few Death Threats Early On.'" *The Guardian*, October 11, 2014. http://www.theguardian.com/music/2014/oct/11/ed-sheeran-interview-death-threats

5. Christina Garibaldi, "Ed Sheeran Never Said He was 'Homeless.'" *MTV News*, October 16, 2014. http://www.mtv.com/news/1965714/ed-sheeran-not-homeless/

Chapter 2. The Rap Solution

1. Andy Welch, "Ed Sheeran: Irish Blood, English Heart," *The Independent*, June 10, 2011. http://www.independent.ie/entertainment/music/ed-sheeran-irish-blood-english-heart-26779193.html

2. Ashley Lee, "Ed Sheeran Gives an Inspiring Speech on Stuttering: 'Embrace Your Weirdness,'" *The Hollywood Reporter*, June 9, 2015. http://www.hollywoodreporter.com/news/ed-sheeran-stutter-speech-embrace-801170

3. Ibid.

4. Ibid.

5. Craig McLean, "The Business of Being Ed Sheeran," *FT Magazine*, December 19, 2014. http://www.ft.com/intl/cms/s/2/0b124842-856a-11e4-ab4e-00144feabdc0.html

6. Jenny Johnston, "Homeless Boy Who Became Britain's Hottest Pop Star . . . and Ed Sheeran Says It's All Thanks to Strict Parents, Messy Break-Ups and Elton John," *The Daily Mail*, October 16, 2014. http://www.dailymail.co.uk/tvshowbiz/article-2796517/homeless-boy-britain-s-hottest-pop-star-ed-sheeran-says-s-thanks-strict-parents-messy-break-ups-elton-john.html

7. Ibid.

8. Lee.

9. Lee.

10. McLean, Craig, "Ed Sheeran Interview: 'I don't make music for critics'. *The Telegraph*, July 16, 2014. http://www.telegraph.co.uk/culture/music/10859780/Ed-Sheeran-interview-I-dont-make-music-for-critics.html

Chapter 3. From the U.K. to the U.S.

1. Andy Welch, "Ed Sheeran: Irish Blood, English Heart," *The Independent*, June 10, 2011. http://www.independent.ie/entertainment/music/ed-sheeran-irish-blood-english-heart-26779193.html

2. Ibid.

3. Sophie Little, "Jamie Foxx Helps Musician Ed Sheeran Land Big Break," *BBC Blast*, July 27, 2010. http://news.bbc.co.uk/local/norfolk/hi/people_and_places/music/newsid_8856000/8856376.stm

4. Erin Whitney, "Here's Why Ed Sheeran Won't Hook Up with Taylor Swift," *The Huffington Post*, May 30, 2015, http://www.huffingtonpost.com/2015/05/30/ed-sheeran-taylor-swift_n_7476274.html

Chapter 4. Astounding Success

1. Andy Welch, "Ed Sheeran: Irish Blood, English Heart," *The Independent*, June 10, 2011. http://www.independent.ie/entertainment/music/ed-sheeran-irish-blood-english-heart-26779193.html

2. James Hibberd, "Ed Sheeran Answers Our 36 Questions," *Entertainment Weekly*, May 20, 2015. http://www.ew.com/article/2015/05/19/ed-sheeran-interview/

3. Ibid.

4. "Ed Sheeran's 'Thinking Out Loud' Sets Chart Record." *BBC News*, June 22, 2015. http://www.bbc.com/news/entertainment-arts-33226978

5. Hibberd.

6. Welch.

Chapter 5. Play It Forward

1. Andy Welch, "Ed Sheeran: Irish Blood, English Heart," *The Independent*, June 10, 2011. http://www.independent.ie/entertainment/music/ed-sheeran-irish-blood-english-heart-26779193.html

2. Andy Morris, "Ed Sheeran Announces Support Acts for Wembley Shows," *Gigwise*, April 9, 2015. http://www.gigwise.com/news/99553/ed-sheeran-wembley-stadium-support-acts-announced

3. Ed Keeble, "Ed Sheeran Launches His Own Record Label Gingerbread," *Gigwise*, March 24, 2015. http://www.gigwise.com/news/99152/ed-sheeran-launches-gingerbread-label-with-jamie-lawson

4. Ilana Kaplan, "Redhead Redemption: Ed Sheeran," *Interview*, n.d. http://www.interviewmagazine.com/music/ed-sheeran#_

Books

Cutler, Bradley. *Ed Sheeran: From Rags to a World-Wide Sensation.* Amazon Digital Services, 2015.

Hays, Craig. *Ed Sheeran: 184 Success Facts.* Emereo Publishing, 2014.

Morreale, Marie. *Ed Sheeran.* Children's Press/Franklin Watts, 2014.

Nolan, David. *Ed Sheeran A+.* John Blake, 2014.

Sheeran, Ed. *Ed Sheeran: A Visual Journey.* Running Press, 2014.

Sheeran, Ed. *Best of Ed Sheeran Songbook.* Hal Leonard, 2014.

Smith, Nancy. *Ed Sheeran Quiz Book: 50 Fun and Fact-Filled Questions about Singer Ed Sheeran.* Amazon Digital Services, 2015.

Winters, Polly. *Ed Sheeran: Odd and Brilliant.* Polly Winters, 2015.

On the Internet

Billboard: "Ed Sheeran"

http://www.billboard.com/artist/276089/ed-sheeran/biography

Bio.com: "Ed Sheeran"

http://www.biography.com/people/ed-sheeran

Ed Sheeran's Facebook Page

https://www.facebook.com/EdSheeranMusic

Ed Sheeran's Official Web Site

http://www.edsheeran.com/

GLOSSARY

bleak (BLEEK)—Without hope, dark, depressing.

chord (KORD)—A combination of three or more musical tones played at the same time.

collaboration (koh-lab-uh-RAY-shun)—Several people working together to create something new.

curator (KYOO-ray-tor)—The person in charge of the items in a museum or art collection.

documentary (dah-kyoo-MEN-tuh-ree)—A movie that explores real people and events without any fictional additions.

justification (jus-tih-fih-KAY-shun)—A reason or explanation.

materialistic (muh-tee-ree-uh-LIS-tik)—Caring greatly for having money or fancy things.

percussively (per-KUH-siv-lee)—In a manner that is quick and loud, with a steady rhythm, like someone hitting a drum.

quirk (KWIRK)—A unique or strange action or behavior.

reassess (ree-uh-SESS)—To think about again.

stutter (STUH-tur)—To speak with involuntary gaps or repeated sounds.